OXFORD
UNIVERSITY PRESS

Looking after Your Dög

Bernie Carr

Contents

Introduction

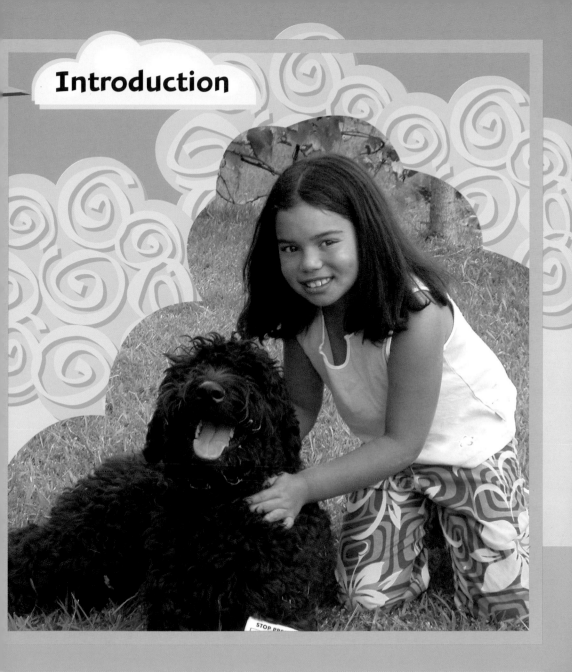

Looking after your dog is important. A dog needs to be looked after every day.

Here are some ways you can look after your dog. This will make your dog happy and healthy.

Feeding

You need to feed your dog every day.
Dogs need to eat well so that they stay
healthy.

Feeding Your Dog
You will need:
a bowl for food
a bowl for water
biscuits
canned dog food

What to do:

1. Open a tin of dog food and put the food in a bowl.
2. Tip biscuits over the dog food.
3. Fill the other bowl with water.
4. Put the bowls out for your dog.

Your dog needs to be able to drink water when it wants to. Make sure there is always water in the water bowl.

Cleaning

You need to keep your dog clean. You need to wash and brush your dog to keep it clean.

Washing Your Dog

You will need:

a hose

a cloth

pet shampoo

a towel

a brush

What to do:

1. Hose your dog down with water.

2. Rub the shampoo into your dog's coat. Remember! Keep the shampoo away from your dog's eyes.

3. Rinse your dog with the hose. Make
   sure you wash off all the shampoo.

4. Dry your dog.

5. Brush your dog.
Wash your dog about twice a year, or
when it is very dirty.
Remember! Buy the shampoo from a vet.

Sleeping

Your dog needs a place to sleep. It needs a place that is warm and dry. A kennel is a good place for a dog to sleep.

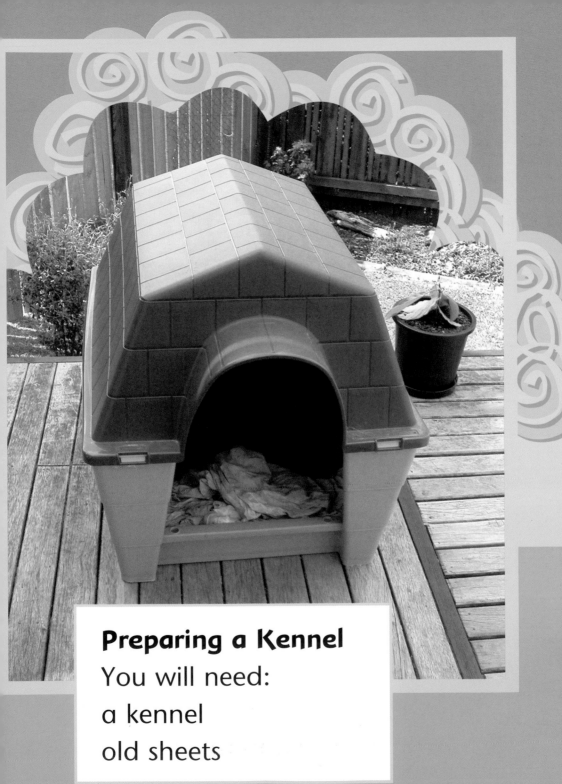

Preparing a Kennel
You will need:
a kennel
old sheets

1. Make sure the kennel is big enough for your dog.
Remember! If your dog is young it will grow bigger.

2. Put the kennel in a place where it is dry.

3. Put the sheets inside the kennel.

4. Let your dog check out the kennel.
Remember! It may take a little while
for your dog to get used to its kennel.

Dogs need exercise to keep them healthy.
Walking your dog will keep it healthy.

Walking Your Dog

You will need:

a lead

a collar

a plastic bag

What to do:
1. Put the collar and the lead on the dog.
2. Walk with your dog on a short lead.
   Remember! If your dog needs to go to
   the toilet, collect it in a plastic bag.

Playing

Dogs need to play. Playing keeps
dogs happy.

Playing with Your Dog

You will need:

a ball

other toys

What to do:

1. Throw a toy for your dog to fetch.

2. Race your dog.

3. Cuddle your dog.

Remember! If you let your dog play with old shoes, it may chew your new shoes.

Index